IMAGES
of America

LOST SERVICE STATIONS OF CENTRAL PENNSYLVANIA

Enos and Anna Miller opened a truck stop in the 1920s. Anna started serving her chicken and waffles in one of the garage bays to those waiting for their trucks to be repaired. As Anna's Pennsylvania Dutch cooking was becoming a larger draw than the truck repair, they opened a small restaurant in 1929. The restaurant is now known as Miller's Smorgasbord, the oldest smorgasbord in Lancaster County. (It is part of Thomas E. Strauss, Incorporated.) Miller's still focuses on Pennsylvania Dutch and classic American cuisine serving Anna's signature chicken and waffles every day. In 2024, Miller's Smorgasbord will celebrate 95 years. (Courtesy Megan Weiss.)

On the Cover: The Sekulski family operated this Sunbury Atlantic service station from 1935 until 2009. It was located at Front Street and Susquehanna Avenue, an area known as "Point Breeze." Family members pictured are, from left to right, sons Charles, Andrew, and Anthony; father A.F.; and Sox the garage dog. (Courtesy Chuck Sekulski.)

IMAGES
of America

Lost Service Stations of Central Pennsylvania

Jimmy Rosen and Emily McCoy
Foreword by Jeff Arch

ISBN 978-1-4671-6122-0

Published by Arcadia Publishing
Charleston, South Carolina

Printed in the United States of America

Library of Congress Control Number: 2023950481

For all general information, please contact Arcadia Publishing:
Telephone 843-853-2070
Fax 843-853-0044
E-mail sales@arcadiapublishing.com

Visit us on the Internet at www.arcadiapublishing.com

To Bob Shultz–thanks for starting us on this service station adventure beginning in 2019. We never thought it would turn into one book, let alone two!

I dedicate this book to my parents for making sure I always had gas money.

–Jimmy

To everyone who's ever listened to my excited chattering about mundane bits of history.

–Emily

CONTENTS

FOREWORD

When Jimmy told me he was doing a book about gas stations, the first thing I asked him about was Oberman's on Maclay Street near Third Street. I asked because Oberman's was the home of the famous "Obiewich"—a greasy mess of a gut bomb, with layers of pepperoni and melted cheese and pizza sauce, all stuffed into an insanely good sub roll—that they made in the back of a gas station. To this day it remains one of the best things I ever remember eating, and legions of locals would agree. I learned about the Obiewich from my father. In the category of things that are terrible for you, it might just have been his favorite thing in the city—and all I can say is thank God my dad grew up in an era where nobody seemed to care about that stuff yet. Today, just reading about this, you should probably call your doctor.

My dad grew up in Harrisburg and lived there all his life. And like a lot of towns our size, kids crossed paths in all kinds of ways. They knew where to get a haircut, a comic book, a bottle of something, or a cigarette. They went to Reservoir Park and Wildwood and City Island and other places they knew, to do things you don't want your parents to see. They were all part of the mix, part of the fabric, of Harrisburg and every place like it.

Except there is no other place like it. Harrisburg is Harrisburg. It's not Albany, it's not Boise or Sacramento or Baton Rouge. Those places have their landmarks I'm sure. They have their neighborhoods, their taverns and diners, their own homegrown joints where whatever they had there was the absolute best.

But they never had an Obiewich. They never went to a Gulf station and came out with a pepperoni sub. Because they'd know if they did, that the argument ended at Third and Maclay Streets.

—Jeff Arch

ACKNOWLEDGMENTS

In late 2019, Bob Shultz, a former employee of the Atlantic Refining Company in Harrisburg, gave author Jimmy Rosen a sizable Atlantic Refining Company image collection, mostly large format negatives. Shultz had discovered a few hundred early images of central Pennsylvania service stations in a closet in the Atlantic Refining office. They were well-preserved, professionally shot images of Atlantic retailers. Most were from the 1920s through the late 1930s and hidden away for decades. Shultz was helping to clear out the office in 1969 after it permanently closed and was instructed to throw everything out—including these negatives. Shultz decided to save them, and they remained safely in his home for the next 50 years. (Shultz's father, Ray "Ben" Shultz, also worked at Atlantic from 1936 to 1972 and assisted in the saving of these images.)

Shultz's generous gift has allowed two books to be created. More than a year was spent identifying the specific locations of the photographs based on clues found within them. Jimmy Rosen, Emily McCoy, and Kurt Harlacher pored over the photographs throughout 2020 using research tools like Newspaper.com, vintage aerial maps, Sanborn fire insurance maps, and a 1939 Harrisburg phone book. Some images were easy to identify while some took a lot of time to figure out. A handful still have not been identified. One of the most rewarding aspects of Rosen's first book, *Got Gas?*, was hearing from people who identified relatives in the book.

Thank you to the Cumberland County Historical Society; West Shore Historical Society; Hershey History Center; Lititz Historical Foundation; Highspire Historical Society; York County History Center; Franklin County Historical Society; AACA Museum, Inc.; Historic Harrisburg Association; and the Pennsylvania Trolley Museum for providing additional photographs for the book.

Thank you to Elizabethtown College professor (and Arcadia book author) Jean-Paul Benowitz for sharing quite a bit of history from Elizabethtown. His student assistant Eric J. Schubert located all the genealogical dates.

We also appreciate the support of authors Jeff Arch, Brian Butko, and Dave Houseal. Thank you to our editor at Arcadia Publishing, Caroline (Anderson) Vickerson, for being very accessible throughout this project.

Unless otherwise noted, all images appear courtesy of author Jimmy Rosen.

Introduction

The invention of the internal combustion engine is arguably one of the top inventions of modern times. As engines improved and automobiles became more prevalent, the need for fueling stations grew, creating the never-before-seen industry of the gas station.

In the early years, refineries primarily focused on producing kerosene, a staple product for heating and lighting since as early as 1500 BCE, along with oils, waxes, and other by-products such as tar and asphalt. At that time, gasoline was considered a waste product, often discarded or sold as a solvent, until the turn of the 20th century when the perfection and popularization of the gas-powered engine increased the demand. Mass production of the Ford Model T, beginning in 1913, allowed many Americans to afford automobiles—cars were not just for the wealthy anymore—and by the 1920s and 1930s, with car ownership booming, gasoline had become the primary product of petroleum companies. In the early years, horse-drawn wagons and tankers often hauled these products—little did the horses know that they would soon be obsolete.

Service station buildings have evolved significantly over the years in terms of architectural design. The first gas stations, or filling stations as they were frequently known, were simple curbside pumps located outside general stores or auto supply retailers. However, as the number of automobiles increased, so did the need for more specialized buildings. The earliest stand-alone gas stations were often small, utilitarian structures designed solely for the purpose of dispensing gasoline. They were typically made of wood and had a single pump and a small office. As competition among oil companies heated up in the 1920s and 1930s, new buildings were stylized to have more distinctive and attractive designs, often mimicking popular styles of the time. For example, many gas stations were designed in the Tudor Revival style, with steeply pitched roofs and false chimneys, or the Spanish Revival or Mission styles, with stucco, parapets, and tile roofs. In the 1930s and 1940s, Art Deco and Streamline Moderne became extremely popular, displaying curves, bold geometric forms, and bright colors. In the 1950s and 1960s, service stations began to adopt a more standardized modern design, typically an oblong box shape with clean lines, flat roofs, and large windows.

For decades, stations were typically full-service, meaning that attendants would pump gas, check oil levels, clean windshields, and sometimes perform minor repairs or maintenance. The transition from full-service to self-service gas stations and convenience stores gained momentum in the 1970s as consumer preferences continued to change. Several factors contributed to this shift. The energy crisis of the 1970s, particularly the Arab Oil Embargo in 1973, led to a significant increase in oil prices and fuel shortages. As a result, consumers became more conscious of fuel consumption and sought ways to save money. Full-service gas stations required staff to provide services such as pumping gas, checking oil, cleaning windshields, and tire maintenance, whereas self-service stations eliminated the need for these additional employees, making them more cost-efficient for gas station owners, who could then pass on the savings to the consumer. As the automotive industry evolved and cars became more reliable, requiring less frequent maintenance, consumers became more comfortable performing basic vehicle maintenance tasks themselves, including pumping gas.

The concept of franchising in the industry became popular in the 1930s. While earlier retailers frequently offered a variety of gas and oil brands for their customers to choose from, franchising flipped that business model to one based on brand loyalty. Oil companies often provided training and support to the franchisees, which could include guidance on how to run the business, marketing support, and technical assistance. Some companies also offered financial help with purchasing equipment or real estate. Furthermore, the oil companies typically took care of the larger strategic decisions, such as pricing and advertising, leaving the franchisees to focus on the day-to-day operations of the service station. This combination of support and independence made franchising an attractive option for many entrepreneurs.

All of this written history of the petroleum industry and service stations is interesting, but for the purpose of this book, it is more about the images. While central Pennsylvania is only a small part of the state and an even smaller fraction of the country, this book will appeal to anyone who fondly remembers their neighborhood service station, no matter where they lived.

One

Early Days in Harrisburg

This is likely the oldest Atlantic Refining photograph in the book, from about 1905. It is from the North Seventh Street campus in Harrisburg. Prior to Atlantic Refining taking over on December 31, 1901, the location was operated by the Capital City Oil Company.

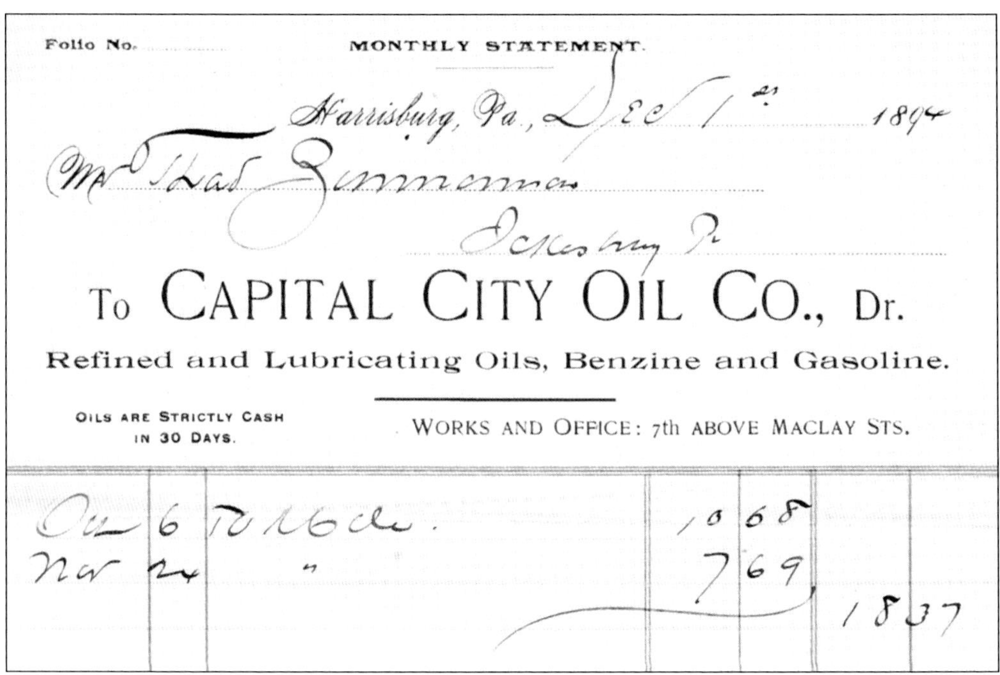

Folio No.

MONTHLY STATEMENT.

Harrisburg, Pa., Dec 1st 1894

Mr Thad Zimmerman

Ickesburg Pa

To CAPITAL CITY OIL CO., Dr.

Refined and Lubricating Oils, Benzine and Gasoline.

OILS ARE STRICTLY CASH IN 30 DAYS.

WORKS AND OFFICE: 7th ABOVE MACLAY STS.

Oct	6	To 1 bbl.	10 68	
Nov	24	"	7 69	18 37

An original 1894 statement and a matching envelope from the Capital City Oil Company were a lucky eBay find. The delivery was to a customer in Ickesburg, Pennsylvania (Perry County). Capital City Oil Company was incorporated on March 2, 1888, and sold to Atlantic Refining on December 31, 1901.

Dated July 12, 1888, this is likely the oldest known original photograph of the Capital City Oil Company. Located in Harrisburg, the capital of Pennsylvania, Capital City Oil Company operated at this location until December 31, 1901.

A large supply of wooden barrels is ready for transporting kerosene to Capitol City Oil Company customers throughout central Pennsylvania. This image is part of a larger panoramic photograph of the campus. It is dated July 12, 1888, and is likely the oldest original photograph of this location.

This was the district office for the Atlantic Refining Company on North Seventh Street in Harrisburg. It was part of a much larger campus that contained giant petroleum storage tanks, warehouses for other petroleum-related products, and stables and living quarters for their workhorses and caretakers. It also contained the bulk of the photographs used for this book, found in a storage closet. The location closed in 1969. Today, the office building remains, but there is no other obvious evidence of a once vital oil business.

This is an Atlantic Refining Company trade show booth in Harrisburg. Items were exhibited to area service station and repair garage owners. Trade shows are a good way for businesses to interact face-to-face with their customers. Based on the Gilbert and Barker pumps displayed, this dates to the early to mid-1920s.

The transition was occurring from horse-drawn wagons to gas-powered vehicles, not just for Atlantic Refining. The delivery truck (right) was owned by C.T. Fernbaugh, a baker located at 1631 North Sixth Street, Harrisburg. They could be dropping off a cake or pie to the Atlantic Refining office. More likely, they were picking up bulk kerosene or fuel oil to take back to their shop, which was only a few blocks away.

This 100-year-old snapshot from North Seventh Street in Harrisburg is historical in the oil industry timeline—not just for Harrisburg but mirrored throughout many parts of the country. A team of horses is pulling a tanker wagon filled with "automobile gasoline." For years, gasoline was a by-product of the refining process, and early on, it was often discarded. With gas-powered vehicles entering the picture, there would be a huge shift toward gasoline sales. Ironically, horses are hauling a product that would eventually make their services obsolete. Soon, Atlantic Refining would not need stables and personnel on-site to care for these horses, which would be a big cost savings for the company. The future would be gas-powered trucks while the horses would enjoy plenty of recreational time frolicking in the meadows.

The Seventh Street complex was the "home base" for Atlantic's fleet of delivery vehicles. The solid wheels on this 1920s truck would have made for a very bumpy ride on the many dirt roads of the era.

This unidentified Atlantic Refining driver takes a break from loading up his tanker for a quick photograph. In addition to gasoline being transported in the large tank, this gentleman will be hauling various bulk motor oils in five-gallon metal containers. The metal containers resemble old milk cans and will be secured on the side of the tanker chassis.

This was another Atlantic Refining tanker truck making area deliveries. This truck, estimated to have been built between 1916 and 1920, was manufactured by the White Motor Company, which became the top truck manufacturer in the country in the years following World War I.

A somewhat subdued driver appears ready to start his day of deliveries. The manufacturer's name is embossed on the top front of the truck's radiator. Though blurry, it appears to be a Federal brand truck. This tanker used solid rubber tires, which were more durable and less likely to puncture or deflate, making them more reliable for the rough road conditions of the time. However, they provided a much bumpier ride and were eventually phased out as pneumatic tire technology improved.

An unidentified Atlantic Refining driver poses with his tanker as he unloads gasoline into an underground storage tank.

An unidentified Atlantic Refining driver is pictured with his tanker at the North Seventh Street district office.

A more modern Atlantic Refining tank truck is shown here filling up at a pipeline terminal. Atlantic built an eight-inch pipeline that extended from Philadelphia to Buffalo. It was completed in 1937 and served the northeastern section of the United States. This photograph is dated April 1954.

Two

Fill 'er Up in Dauphin County

Edward S. Swartz started Swartz Service and Electric in the mid-to-late 1930s. Soon afterward, it offered Esso brand gasoline with pumps along the curb in Hummelstown. The distinctive oval pole sign was welcoming to travelers passing through the Hummelstown town square. During part of his youth, former Speaker of the US House of Representatives Newt Gingrich lived in an apartment upstairs. Though long closed, the building remains today, entombed in vinyl siding. The Swartz family purchased Indian Echo Cave in 1942 (later renamed Indian Echo Caverns), a popular attraction in Pennsylvania. The family is still involved in that business today. (Courtesy Miller Library, Pennsylvania Trolley Museum Archive.)

As Milton Hershey's chocolate empire grew, he saw the need for an efficient trolley system. Trolleys not only transported workers to Hershey's factories but also brought large quantities of milk from area farms. The location of this photograph is 23 East Main Street, Hummelstown, and is dated August 3, 1938. Three "curb pumps" are visible on the left side of the image, offering Atlantic and Sico gasoline. (Courtesy Miller Library, Pennsylvania Trolley Museum Archive.)

J.A. Stein owned and operated this elegant-looking gas station and repair garage at 6460 Jonestown Road in Lower Paxton Township, a suburb of Harrisburg. The building has been well preserved, including the Spanish-style tiled roof. It is used as a dental office today—one can joke it is still a "filling" station. Shown here are two different eras of the building; an addition was put on later to service more vehicles.

Elizabeth Rodkey means business. She and her grandson Eddie Latsha are posing in front of a tall, "clock face" Atlantic gas pump (Wayne model 866). The location is the E.J. Rodkey service station at Sixth Street and Linglestown Road in uptown Harrisburg. In the 1940s, the business was leased to Lou Johnson, and it was then known as Lou's Service Station for many years. After nearly 90 years, the building remains today. The last few businesses to occupy the modest brick structure have all been hair salons.

Built in 1929, the Fort Hunter Service Station/Tourist Camp at 5415 North Front Street, Harrisburg, was owned and operated by the Martin family and served the communities between Harrisburg and Amity Hall, fitting nicely into the growing trend of automobile travel for pleasure. In 1946, the Martins renovated the station to include a coffee, gift, and antique shop. They sold the station in 1955 to Aero Oil Company, which leased it to the Neidig family. The Neidigs carried Atlantic products and operated the station until 1963, when the planning of the "River Relief Route," or US Route 22/322 as it is known today, drastically cut down on the amount of traffic passing by this lovely station. (Courtesy Fort Hunter Mansion and Park.)

Evelyn Neidig is shown here getting payment from a customer. She was often seen pumping gas, checking oil, and filling tires. (Courtesy the Neidig family.)

Early service stations were a hodgepodge of structures. There was no uniformity in the locations in the early years. This 1922 image of Eshelman's Garage on Derry Road and Trinidad Avenue served Hershey. From left to right are Irvin Deets, Lloyd Loy, Jake Eshelman, and Daniel Yost. It seems there was some confusion about how to spell "Eshelman" on the advertising signs. (Courtesy Hershey History Center.)

Of the hundreds of images in the author's collection, the New Willow Brook service station was the only one to advertise dancing. A 1930 newspaper advertisement also advertised "midget golf." The location was along Route 230, one-half mile east of Middletown.

Joseph E. Solomon owned and operated this modest coal, wood, and stone business located at 987 South Front Street, Steelton. Beginning in the early 1920s as the Steelton Coal Company, the business sold a few different grades of gasoline as well as kerosene. Sadly, Joseph died in 1936 at age 42, and the business closed soon after. His widow, Rose, managed to open a successful department store in Steelton (Solomon's Department Store), which stayed in business until 1971. (Courtesy Michael Solomon.)

Nothing remains of this dazzling service station owned by H.C. Emerick. It was located along US Route 22/322, southeast of Dauphin. Over the years, the highway has gone through major reconstruction and realignments with additional driving lanes added. All structures along the route were razed.

This 1945 image captures the sunset days of the trolley during the blossoming era of personal automobile ownership. Trolley No. 21 is heading westbound from Palmyra toward Hershey, along old Route 322. There is a rural Atlantic service station off to the right. Winding farm fields still make up a large part of Pennsylvania's landscape, but the days of the trolley are long gone. (Courtesy Miller Library, Pennsylvania Trolley Museum Archive.)

The V.D. Leisure building at Twentieth Street and Derry Street in Harrisburg was a fine one in its day. Opened in 1928 by Vernon D. Leisure, president of the General Tire Sales Company, the complex remains today but with no evidence of the past service station activity. Like so many of the pictures in this book, the gas pumps, signs, air meters, etc. are highly prized by petroliana collectors today.

Cyrus "Cy" Keefer owned and operated this Gulf station in Highspire on the northwest corner of Second Street and White House Lane, across from the Twin Kiss ice cream stand. Keefer opened his first gas station while still in high school in 1947. At one point, he had a contract with the airport and was open 24 hours a day for AAA towing. The service station was sold to Turkey Hill after Keefer passed at age 51 in 1980. (Both, courtesy Lorri Keefer Siffin.)

Shreve Service Company was a large and beautiful brick structure, meticulously maintained with several gas pumps along the curb. This uptown area of Harrisburg, Pennsylvania, has completely changed with virtually all of the residences and commercial buildings having been leveled. The address was 1618 North Sixth Street, Harrisburg.

The Shreve Service Company was located at 1618 North Sixth Street in the uptown area of Harrisburg. That area has gone through a total makeover in the last few decades, with most of the old structures gone after becoming dilapidated, including the once beautiful Shreve building.

Around 1920, Fred Nelson and his son Harold opened Nelson's Cloverly Service on the northwest corner of Seventeenth and Paxton Streets, Harrisburg. At one point, the Nelsons owned all four corners with a variety of businesses, including a miniature golf course on the northeast corner. Nelson's daughter Ruth operated Boots Confectionery at one of the properties. The Nelsons owned two homes off Paxton Street, living in one. Sadly, they lost almost everything in the Great Depression. (Courtesy J. Michael Davis.)

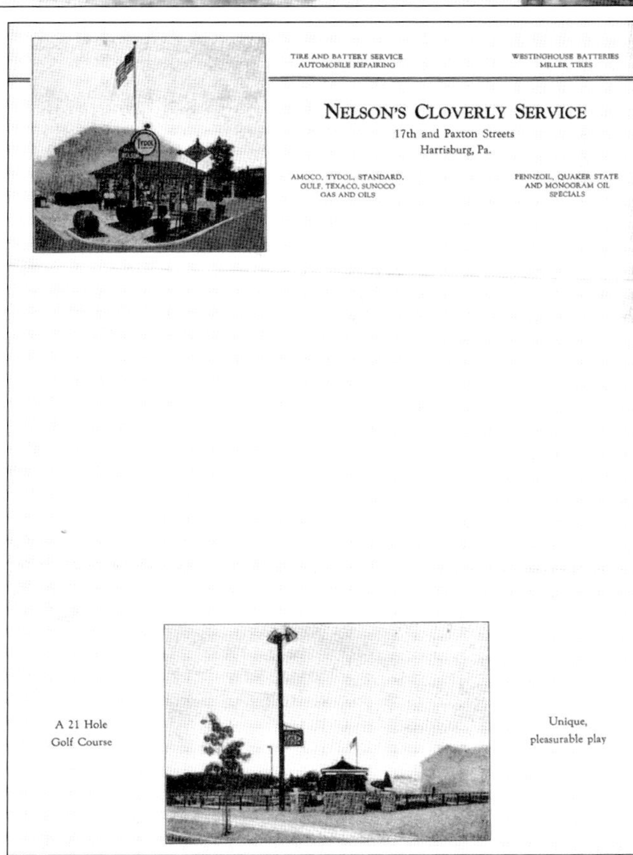

TIRE AND BATTERY SERVICE
AUTOMOBILE REPAIRING

WESTINGHOUSE BATTERIES
MILLER TIRES

NELSON'S CLOVERLY SERVICE

17th and Paxton Streets
Harrisburg, Pa.

AMOCO, TYDOL, STANDARD, GULF, TEXACO, SUNOCO GAS AND OILS

PENNZOIL, QUAKER STATE AND MONOGRAM OIL SPECIALS

A 21 Hole Golf Course

Unique, pleasurable play

This is an original letterhead from Nelson's Cloverly Service located at Seventeenth and Paxton Streets, Harrisburg. (Courtesy J. Michael Davis.)

J.H. "Fat" Miller's store was located by the toll house where East Derry Road comes into East Chocolate Avenue, Hershey. This area is known as the "triangle." Miller's building is no longer there, but the tollhouse exists, having been moved 100 yards north in 1915 to 1702 Palm Street.

This location was at the 2700 block of Walnut Street, in a suburb of Harrisburg known as Penbrook. At one time, it was the major route out of Harrisburg heading east toward Allentown, Pennsylvania. (A street marker for Route 43 is shown. That route number is obsolete today.) One of the interesting features of this photograph is all the brands of gasoline offered at this location. This is unheard of today.

The Parkside, named for nearby Reservoir Park, opened at 2007–2009 State Street in Harrisburg in the early 1920s. In the 1930s, it added food sales to its business, beginning the era of the Park Side Café that would last into the 2010s. The full transition from fuel to food was made in the late 1940s when the overhang was enclosed to create a larger dining area.

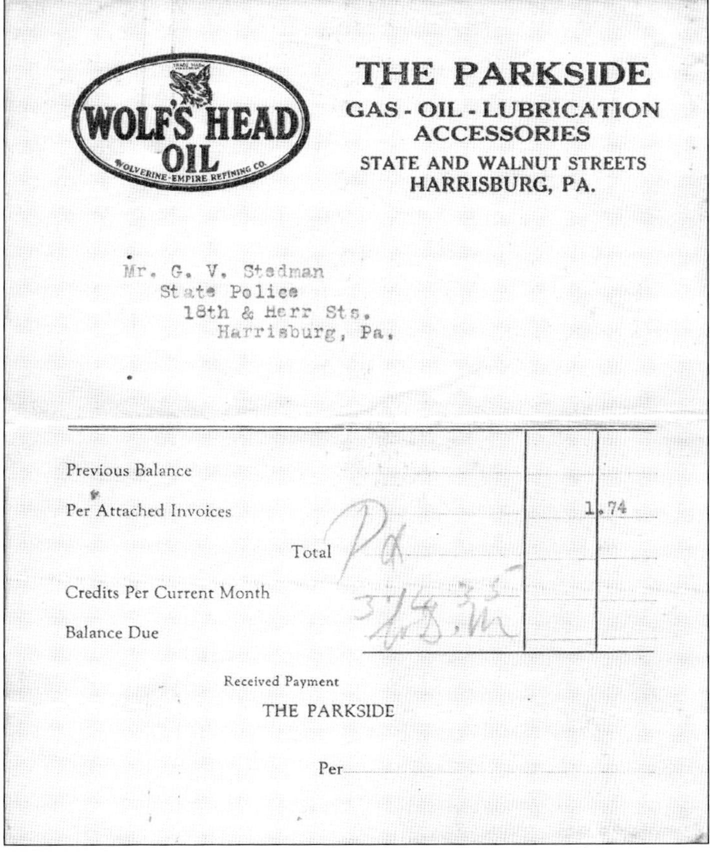

WOLF'S HEAD OIL
WOLVERINE-EMPIRE REFINING CO.

THE PARKSIDE
GAS - OIL - LUBRICATION
ACCESSORIES
STATE AND WALNUT STREETS
HARRISBURG, PA.

Mr. G. V. Stedman
State Police
18th & Herr Sts.
Harrisburg, Pa.

Previous Balance		
Per Attached Invoices		1.74
Total		
Credits Per Current Month		
Balance Due		

Received Payment
THE PARKSIDE

Per

This is an original statement from the Parkside when it did work for the nearby state police barracks.

The original Fawber's Garage and gas station was started by Russell U. Fawber in the 1930s. It was located on a hill at 4910 Jonestown Road (US Route 22) east of Harrisburg in the suburb of Colonial Park. The building and hill no longer exist. (Courtesy Patricia Fawber Nolan and James Fawber.)

In the early 1940s construction started on a new Fawber's Garage and Esso Station at 4610 Jonestown Road. The new location also included a 24-hour restaurant, a Hudson dealership, a used car lot, a taxi service, and a motel. Jonestown Road, designated as US Route 22, was the main highway to New York City and therefore an excellent location for all aspects of the business. The garage and motel buildings still exist but have been converted for modern use. (Courtesy Patricia Fawber Nolan and James Fawber.)

As competition among oil companies heated up, the architectural design of gas stations began to evolve. Companies started to realize that the design of their stations could be a distinguishing factor, attracting more customers. This led to the adoption of various architectural styles, with gas stations being designed to mimic popular styles of the time. This Harrisburg location was patterned after the Spanish Colonial Revival style, employing features such as clay tile roofing, a smooth stucco exterior, and wrought iron hardware. This location was at the southeast corner of Cameron and Herr Streets, Harrisburg.

Early gas stations, or filling stations as they were known, were often just simple curbside pumps located outside mom-and-pop neighborhood stores. As the popularity of automobiles grew, the demand for fuel increased, leading to the development of stand-alone gas stations.

Auto garages offered basic services and repairs on most vehicles. Oil changes and new tires were popular. This Atlantic Lubrication building was on the same property as one of the octagon-shaped filling stations. The left side of the image shows a partially obscured word painted on the building behind the Atlantic Lubrication garage. It turned out to be "carburetor," which helped identify the address of this image as 230 South Cameron Street, Harrisburg.

The location of this Tydol service station was a mystery for a while. Upon further investigation of the negative, a distinctive building was revealed on the right side. It was the newly opened Farm Show Complex in Harrisburg. This clue enabled the exact location to be determined. The address was 2030 North Cameron Street, the southwest corner of Cameron and Maclay Streets.

The majority of the Atlantic Refining service stations in this book were not marked with street addresses. Some detective work was needed to identify the locations. Many photographs offered clues, and some clues were more obvious than others. The proprietor's name above the doorway (shown here) made it easy to research that name and find a location. This was Sixteenth and State Streets in Harrisburg.

This three-story brick and frame building at 301 Cumberland Street in Harrisburg was severely gutted by a fast-moving fire on February 19, 1936. It housed the repair garage and Atlantic Refining dealer of Earl A. Wagner, C.J. Blair Printing, and the Myers Manufacturing Company. The cause of the fire was attributed to an overheated chimney in the tire shop and damage was estimated at nearly $10,000. (Courtesy Dave Houseal.)

This is Derry Street between Seventeenth and Eighteenth Streets, Harrisburg. Unfortunately, there are no remnants of the early Capital Gas service station in front of the imposing brick building. But the brick building has a notable past. A century ago, it housed an ice-cream and candy company called Hershey Bros. Chocolates, which was not related to Milton Hershey's chocolate empire in nearby Hershey. Today, Milton Hershey's multinational chocolate/candy business is officially known as the Hershey Company and the former Hershey Bros. Chocolates is Hershey Creamery (also known as Hershey's Ice Cream). A faded Hershey Bros. sign is still visible, painted high up on the brick facade.

The partially obscured name on the lower-right side of this building was a clue that enabled the location to be identified as 672 Second Street, Highspire. The proprietor, H.C. "Henry" Wallinger, started the gas station and lunch counter business sometime between 1923 and 1927. This early-1930s photograph shows several gas pumps out front with multiple brands, including Texaco, Amoco, Tydol, Esso, Sunoco, and Atlantic. Prior to the 1950s and 1960s, it was common for gas stations to offer multiple brands of gasoline. The location later became McCauley's in the 1940s in a greatly expanded two-story building with a flat roof. It was a very popular place with a restaurant and pool room upstairs. (Courtesy Highspire Historical Society.)

This image of the Plasterer's Square Deal Station, located at 570 Second Street, Highspire, was taken around 1925. A later Plasterer's Garage was built in the same area in the newly developed east end of the Highspire Borough. (Courtesy Highspire Historical Society.)

The architectural design of early gas stations is a fascinating study of how functionality and aesthetics can merge to create structures that not only serve a practical purpose but also contribute to the visual appeal of the urban landscape. At one time, the Harrisburg city limits had three octagon-shaped Atlantic Refining service station buildings. All three are shown here. Unfortunately, none exist today. This location was at Seventeenth and Derry Streets, Harrisburg.

This is a May 22, 1922, advertisement from the *Harrisburg Telegraph* newspaper announcing the grand opening of this octagon-shaped Atlantic station at Seventeenth and Derry Streets.

These are the other two octagon-shaped Atlantic stations. Above is North Third and Harris Streets, Harrisburg. Below is Stickel's Atlantic, located at 236 South Cameron Street, Harrisburg.

Kehres Atlantic Service was located at 189 Second Street, Highspire. This photograph was taken on July 16, 1939, from the front platform of the last trolley on the Steelton-Highspire-Middletown line. This explains the crowd of people, some of whom can be seen aiming their cameras at the oncoming trolley. The original Highspire State Bank is the wedge-shaped brick building on the left of the photograph. The building that housed Kehres Atlantic Service was razed after the Agnes flood of 1972. (Courtesy Highspire Historical Society.)

The proprietor of this Harrisburg gas station and bar had a famous name: W. Shakespeare. Playwright William Shakespeare lived from 1564 to 1616, so there was no chance he was part of this operation located at 1843 North Cameron Street, Harrisburg. "To beer or not to beer?" would have been a memorable tagline for the business.

This beautiful Sinclair service station was located at Paxton and Vine Streets in Shipoke, a Harrisburg neighborhood south of downtown. This area is known for its historic homes, community events, and location along the Susquehanna River.

Simple in design with a stepped parapet facade, this early station is an example of a classic "garage-style" building. One can still find this building, although it has been repurposed, in the 3900 block of Jonestown Road, Harrisburg (Lower Paxton Township).

The Hain brothers stand proudly outside their service station. The oil racks and window display are well-organized, possibly for a grand opening. An eye-catching kerosene pump is located at the left corner of the building—nearly 10 feet tall.

Robert Oberman Sr. owned and operated Oberman's Gulf station and the Treat Shoppe Restaurant at Third and Maclay Streets in Harrisburg. He was injured during his military service and was disabled. He wore a back brace for decades, though it did not keep him from years of working at his service station. Oberman's Gulf was known throughout central Pennsylvania for the "Obiewich," a specialty sandwich made there for years. Jeff Arch, *Sleepless in Seattle* screenwriter and former Harrisburg resident, would go there as a boy with his father. (He mentions it in the foreword.) This June 1969 photograph is the only known image of the location. (Courtesy Robert Oberman Jr.)

D.L. Warner stands proudly in the doorway of his neighborhood Atlantic station located at Sixth and Reily Streets, Harrisburg. There is a framed "Certificate of Merit" hanging in the window dated 1937, which is consistent with many of the Atlantic Refining photographs in this book.

Warner's polished location was an asset to the neighborhood even though it was too small to have a garage bay or outside lift for repairs. Hidden below the left Lee Tire sign is a short cabinet-style dual gas pump. This station offered White Flash and Ethyl grades of gasoline, likely utilizing this style of pump due to the limited space.

Opened in 1924, this Atlantic station at Second and Verbeke Streets in Harrisburg was patterned after the Spanish Colonial Revival style. Some of the most visible features were a clay tile roof and a smooth stucco exterior. Pictured right is an advertisement from the *Harrisburg Telegraph* published on April 17, 1924.

OPEN

A New Atlantic Station

ATLANTIC GASOLINE

Second and Verbeke Sts.

DRIVE into this new Atlantic Station—established for your convenience—and see the latest in service station facilities. Atlantic Service is the modern way of selling gasoline. It marks the day when a gallon of gasoline has more than a money equivalent-an extra measure of return—when served with consideration for your convenience, comfort and the value of your time. It represents the thought and effort of an organization constantly striving to increase its usefulness to the motoring and truck operating public.

Other Atlantic Service Stations in Harrisburg are at Seventeenth and Derry Sts. and Cameron and Kittatinny Sts.

Atlantic Service Means:

ACCURACY. Pumps are daily inspected for absolute accuracy.

SAFETY. The fullest measures of safety and convenience are provided. Wide driveways; no crowding; no backing out.

PROMPTNESS. The number of pumps and their [illegible] to assure quick service and getaway.

CLEANLINESS. The spick-and-span appearance of Atlantic Stations appeals to the discriminating motorist.

COURTESY. Atlantic Service begins and ends with courtesy.

SERVICE WITHOUT OBLIGATION. Atlantic attendants do not expect and will not accept gratuities.

ATLANTIC
GASOLINE
Puts Pep in Your Motor

Many early gasoline proprietors simply added curb pumps to an existing storefront, as seen here at 407–409 Walnut Street in downtown Harrisburg. After refueling their cars, customers could walk a few feet and refuel their bodies at the Star Quick Lunch next door. The building remains today but without any hint of its early years as a service station.

This beautiful Spanish Revival–style Atlantic station greeted travelers and city workers coming into downtown Harrisburg via Second and Mulberry Streets. Blending with the decor are short, ornate, cabinet-type gas pumps; an attendant can be seen using one of them to fuel a car.

Decades ago, car dealerships were a natural location for having retail gas pumps like this Chevrolet location in Middletown, Pennsylvania. The rise of self-service convenience stores, which began in the 1970s and gained momentum throughout the 1980s and 1990s, was one factor that shifted the gasoline business away from car dealers. As the name suggests, convenience stores are typically more conveniently located, often situated along major roads or highways. They offer easy access for customers to fill up their vehicles.

This Ford dealership (North Mountain Road and Raspberry Lane, Linglestown) was founded by J.W. Ebersole, who started his career in the automotive industry in the early 1920s. He initially worked as a mechanic before opening his own service station. In 1927, he expanded his business to include a Ford dealership. The three-story building to the left is the former Eagle Inn, still open today and known as the Eagle Bar and Restaurant.

The William Penn Service Station was located at 295 East Main Street, Hummelstown. It was likely named after the William Penn Highway, which encompassed Main Street and spanned from Pittsburgh to New York.

This location was the 100 block of West Chocolate Avenue, Hershey. The large pole sign advertised three different brands of gasoline: Tydol, Atlantic, and Amoco. The associated gas pumps were disguised in ornate cabinets to blend in with the surroundings and not detract from the aesthetic of Hershey's quaint Chocolate Avenue business district.

"The architecture of Gulf stations is designed to fit into the surroundings and beautify, rather than disfigure the location," said a Mr. Whitemarsh, local manager of the Gulf Refining Company. This was very evident at this location (Second and Sayford Streets, Harrisburg).

Beginning in 1916, Jacob C. Hess set up shop at 18 East Derry Road, Hershey. He was originally a butcher but began assembling Ford Model Ts. His son Irvin J. Hess would eventually take over. A small sign at the Derry Road location indicated Pontiac and Oakland automobile sales and service along with Atlantic gas and oil. (Photograph from AACA Museum, Inc.; courtesy Jim Hess.)

The business grew and moved around the early 1920s to 313 West Chocolate Avenue, Hershey. By then, it was known as J.C. Hess Ford. (Photograph from AACA Museum, Inc.; courtesy Jim Hess.)

The c. 1937 gas pumps were placed out front of the Hess Ford dealership (313 West Chocolate Avenue, Hershey). The fuel area was replaced with an expanded car lot by 1959. (Photograph from AACA Museum, Inc.; courtesy Jim Hess.)

Prior to the 1950s, it was common for gas stations to offer multiple brands of gasoline. However, as oil companies grew and started to franchise their operations, they began to require gas stations to sell only their brand of gasoline. This trend continued, and by the late 20th century, most gas stations were selling only one brand of gasoline. This location was Twenty-Fourth and Walnut Streets, Penbrook—a suburb of Harrisburg.

This 1930s image was included in the book *Got Gas?* but the location was not known at the time. After further research, the address was discovered (317 Second Street, Highspire). In the 1950s, there was a Merit gas station at this location according to the Highspire Historical Society.

This American Oil Company (Amoco) filling station was at Nineteenth and Derry Streets (west corner), Harrisburg. Advanced detective work was needed to identify this location. The Route 230 sign attached to the lamppost was the primary clue to get started. Old city maps and a 1939 Harrisburg phone book assisted greatly.

Travelers passing 1720 South Cameron Street, Steelton, might be confused by this sign. Is it Capital Gas or Capitol Gas?

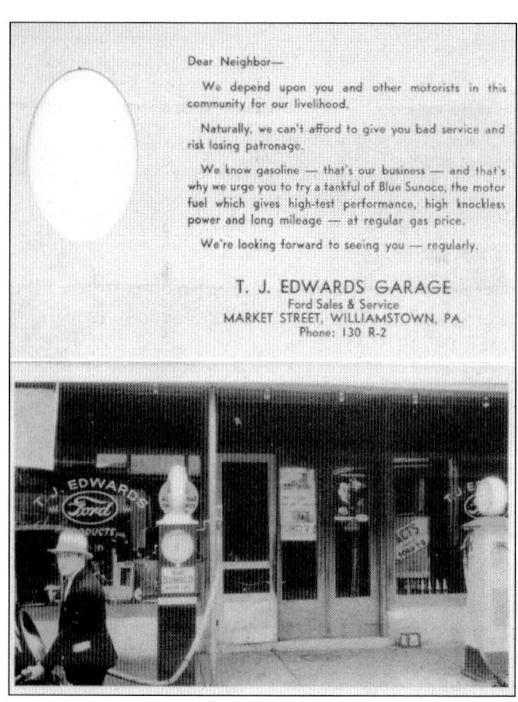
Dear Neighbor—

We depend upon you and other motorists in this community for our livelihood.

Naturally, we can't afford to give you bad service and risk losing patronage.

We know gasoline — that's our business — and that's why we urge you to try a tankful of Blue Sunoco, the motor fuel which gives high-test performance, high knockless power and long mileage — at regular gas price.

We're looking forward to seeing you — regularly.

T. J. EDWARDS GARAGE
Ford Sales & Service
MARKET STREET, WILLIAMSTOWN, PA.
Phone: 130 R-2

This original folding advertising piece featured T.J. Edwards, Market Street, Williamstown. Opening in 1928, Edwards was a Ford dealership and Sunoco-brand gasoline retailer. (Courtesy Williamstown Historical Society.)

The location of this Gulf filling station was Seventh Street, looking north from Forster Street. A small sign for Kimmel's Garage was a helpful clue for determining the location.

Before chain motels and hotels, weary travelers often stayed in roadside cottages. These were usually basic one-room structures, separate from the main building. Early cottages had no running water; bathrooms were nearby outhouses. The proprietor often lived with his family on-site and had food service in a modest dining room. After guests "fueled up" on breakfast, they could often fuel up their cars with convenient gas pumps out front. This location was along Route 230 (2495 East Harrisburg Pike, Middletown). The main building still remains and is open as a bar and restaurant. (No cabins remain.) (Courtesy Walt Balmer.)

In 1926, Preston V. Troutman built a general store and service station in Pillow, Pennsylvania, along Route 225. For a time, it was referred to as Troutman's Gap. There was also a small restaurant and candy shop inside. Troutman also had a heating oil business at the same location, Troutman's Oil Service. It was an Atlantic Refining dealer. Sons Glenn, Richard, and Joy Troutman worked in the family business started by their father. (Courtesy Ann Troutman Long and Karen Troutman Kocher.)

Joy Troutman is shown here filling up his Buick at Troutman's Gap service station (February 1958.) He bought a new Buick every year, in either green or blue. His daughters Karen (left) and Ann (right) enjoyed rides with their father. (Courtesy Ann Troutman Long and Karen Troutman Kocher.)

For the first time in the company's history, in May 1942 women were employed as attendants at this American Oil Company (Amoco) station at Front and Verbeke Streets in Harrisburg. They were Hilda Hackenberg and Mrs. Phillip Spaid. "If the total experiment in the employment of women is successful, the plan will be expanded to other of the company stations," said H.L. Schriver, branch manager. (Courtesy Historic Harrisburg Association.)

C.S. Bushey and H.C. Whitcomb were proprietors of this location (10 South Cameron Street, Harrisburg.) Prior to moving there, Bushey-Whitcomb was located several blocks south at 200 South Cameron Street, Harrisburg. The business had opened originally in 1927. The new location (shown here) opened in April 1933. An unrelated business, Harrisburg Autoparts Company, can be seen in the background and supplied parts for many area service stations and repair garages. An original 1956 invoice (seen below) is made out to L.L. Landis service station in Mount Pleasant Mills. Landis is mentioned more in chapter six.

CARLISLE
CHAMBERSBURG
LEBANON

HARRISBURG AUTOPARTS COMPANY
DISTRIBUTORS OF
PARTS . . SUPPLIES . . ACCESSORIES . . EQUIPMENT
HARRISBURG, PA.

LEWISTOWN
SUNBURY
YORK

SOLD TO L L LANDIS SERV. STA.
MT. PLEASANT MILLS PA.

INVOICE DATE 10-5-56 | INVOICE NO. S 59309
STORE SBY | WRITTEN BY KERN
SHIP VIA | SHIP WHEN | YOUR ORDER NO. | ORDER DATE 10-4-56 | TERMS 2% | SALESMAN 11

B/O	ORDERED	SHIPPED	STOCK NO.	DESCRIPTION	LIST PRICE	NET PRICE OR DISC.	TOTAL
	2	2	509	E.R. BATTERY	.90	.61	1.22
1	1	0	770	UNITY		N/C	
				~~LESS 772 UNITY~~			

FROM INVOICE NO. AND DATE | REC'D BY | SALES TAX

CR. APPD. BY | FILLED BY | PACKED BY | DATE SHIPPED 10-5-56 | DELIVERED BY | TOTAL 1.22

FORM NO. 41

THIS IS YOUR INVOICE

The firehouse at 2006 State Street was built in 1928 for the Pleasant View Fire Company No. 16. With the demise of volunteer firemen, by the 1970s it became an all-career station housing Squad 1, one of the busiest fire companies in Central Pennsylvania at that time. It closed in 1978 when the apparatus floor was deemed unfit for the heavy truck assigned there. (Courtesy Dave Houseal.)

Beginning in 1936, Martin and Marlin Duey operated Duey Brothers Service Station (144 North Front Street, Steelton). In 1941, the service station had the unfortunate distinction of being burglarized six times. Martin Duey died in October 1946. There was not much history about the station after that date, which suggests it was possibly sold or closed.

R.T. Shertzer operated the Shellsville Garage at 9231 Jonestown Road, Shellsville (East Hanover Township). Although the sign says "Standard," the pumps offer multiple varieties of both Standard and Atlantic gasoline.

At one time, the 100 block of Market Street in downtown Harrisburg was home to a handful of automobile-related businesses. Naturally, they offered curbside pumps for convenient fill-ups.

Food, bowling, camping, auto repair, and four different brands of gasoline—Dave Ream's had it all. This garage was located on East Chocolate Avenue at Edwin Street, Hershey.

Located a few miles west of Dauphin (Speeceville) along US Routes 22 and 322 was this curiously named roadside business, Rotary Gas Garden. Rotary Gas Gardens were service stations that operated from the 1920s to the 1950s. They were related to Socony, which stands for Standard Oil Company of New York. Charles J. Griffith Sr. ran the station in Speeceville for 29 years before he retired. During World War II, his wife, Irma, ran the station when everything was rationed. She also operated the lunch counter, which included making soup and sandwiches for hungry customers. The old station was torn down around 1955, and a new one was built in its place. Unfortunately, nothing remains of the Rotary except memories. (Courtesy Sam Griffith.)

This Atlantic station in Grantville was perfectly situated for business. Prominently located right in the center of the village, its customers would have included locals, hotel guests, and the many travelers passing by on the William Penn Highway.

Looking east along Routes 22 and 322 toward Harrisburg, this view is from a lookout tower on the grounds of the Water Gap Lunch and Service Station. The tower was moved to the property in the 1940s as an attraction for the business. In 1999, it was relocated to the Old Sled Works property in Duncannon where it still stands today. (It is not open to the public.)

The Sweigard family owned and operated this country store and Gulf gas station from 1941 to 1973 in Matamoras. The address is 3266 Peters Mountain Road, Halifax. (Courtesy Cindy Rae Sweigard Tobias.)

This early photograph shows the Highspire Garage at 186 Second Street, with employees proudly standing outside the wooden bay doors. The Gross family operated this service station alongside a car dealership for many years before closing to expand their hardware business, which remained until 1997. (Courtesy of Highspire Historical Society.)

Tom Black had two repair garage locations in Harrisburg. One was at 205 South Seventeenth Street and the other (shown here) was at 116–120 South Eighteenth Street. Based on many of his 1930s *Harrisburg Telegraph* newspaper advertisements, Black specialized in automobile greasing: "Correct lubrication saves repair bills. Mighty few garages are equipped to properly lubricate your car, few mechanics have the knowledge to do a thorough job. We are experts."

Determining the site of this 1950s-era Gulf station was made easy by having a street sign prominently displayed in the picture. The location is North Sixth Street and Schuylkill Street, Harrisburg.

Three

Refuel in Cumberland County

Onlookers survey the wreckage of a Pomeroy's delivery truck at the Keystone Super Service Esso Station at Thirty-Second and Market Streets, Camp Hill, on November 3, 1950. Five people were injured in the crash, which occurred when the delivery truck swerved to avoid stopped traffic ahead. (Photograph by Richard Heintzelman; courtesy of Cumberland County Historical Society.)

Salteau "S.J." Quigley, always known as "Salty," was born in Mechanicsburg in 1914. He moved to Lemoyne as a young man and attended Lemoyne High School until 1929. Home problems caused him to take a job full-time at the local Standard Oil station. That place later became the S.J. Quigley Esso gas station in the 1930s. He retired in 1979, and the gas station was torn down. During Salty's career, the world went to war. He was drafted in 1942 but was never called to serve. One of the reasons he was deferred was that his Esso station was a relay stop for Associate Transport. Being

at the intersection of Routes 11 and 15, the stop was on the way from Oak Ridge, Tennessee, to New York. The trucks were carrying secret cargo and were part of the Manhattan Project (the secret operation that built the atomic bomb). During his tenure, his business went from an important route for the Florida/Canadian trade to a neighborhood center, always with a smile and a clean Bon Ami windshield, a trademark at Fifth and Market Street, Lemoyne. (Courtesy of Jim Quigley.)

A proud S.J. Quigley stands ready for his grand opening at Fifth and Market Streets in Lemoyne. This original photograph is from the early 1930s. (Courtesy Jim Quigley.)

S.J. Quigley's service station enjoyed sharing special celebrations with the community. This is its 30th anniversary (1961).

Paxton's Grocery and Atlantic Station was located at 923 North West Street in Carlisle, Pennsylvania. Gas pumps were typically out front, often with a kerosene pump at the side of the building. A few Coca-Cola signs add a bit of decor to this simple location. (Courtesy Cumberland County Historical Society.)

Owned and operated by Earl W. Frycklund, this Esso service station, restaurant, and miniature golf course provided fuel, food, and family entertainment for years. It was located at Walnut Bottom Road and College Street in Carlisle. The car is a 1941 Ford station wagon; the photograph is from around 1942. (Courtesy Cumberland County Historical Society.)

When Joel T. Miller was 19 years old, he wanted to lease this gas station on Bridge Street in New Cumberland from Atlantic Refining. Miller was concerned that Atlantic would not let him sign a contract because of his age, so he signed the contract using his older brother's name, Oliver. This is why the sign at the station reads, "Oliver Miller." Oliver was stationed overseas in the military and had no idea this occurred. The service station was very successful for many years, even with this hidden secret. (Courtesy the Miller family.)

Beginning in 1928, Herman L. Mills owned several gas stations in Maryland and southern Pennsylvania, including this location at the 200 block of North Earl Street, Shippensburg. A shrewd businessman, Mills was also involved in the coal business and grocery business at various times, known for undercutting his competitors. He disliked bureaucrats and often faced conflicts with the government due to his unorthodox style of business, openly violating rules set during the Great Depression. Ironically, Mills got into politics and was mayor of Hagerstown, Maryland, from 1949 to 1953.

Shown is Bruce Larson's hot rod "Mr. Clean" at the former Miller's Mobil gas station (Eighteenth and Market Streets) in Camp Hill. In 1960, Larson was known to hang out there along with other car enthusiast friends. Larson, who was born in Camp Hill and made Dauphin his racing base, is widely regarded as one of the founding fathers of drag racing's most popular class, funny cars, back in the 1960s. (Courtesy Bruce Larson.)

Like many early gas stations, this building served multiple needs within its community. This July 1925 photograph shows Albert E. Enck (left) and Reily B. Urich (right) outside the combination gas station/post office/general store in Churchtown (also known as Allen). (Courtesy Cumberland County Historical Society.)

F.E. Goodhart (left) and his mechanic Charley (right, his name embroidered above his shirt pocket) stand proudly in front of their newly opened Atlantic service station at Seventeenth and Market Streets, Camp Hill. A mid-1930s poster in the window (lower right) advertises an upcoming annual fair sponsored by the local fire department.

This was the Willow Filling Station, Carlisle. After his death in 1938, original owner Levi Hertzler had made arrangements to pass the business to his son L. Richard "Dick" Hertzler.

Pride in ownership is evident in the neatly organized displays outside the Willow Filling Station at Hanover and Willow Streets, Carlisle. Owner Dick Hertzler (left) and his mechanic, known only as Paul (right), are shown here, eager to serve their customers.

The Downtown Service Station in Carlisle was opened in 1938 as an L-shaped complex with entrances on both Louther and Pitt Streets. Seen here is the building at 23 North Pitt Street. (Courtesy Cumberland County Historical Society.)

This was the Sunny-Side Service Station and Tourist Home on Route 11 near the Carlisle Barracks. The image dates to around 1945. (Courtesy Cumberland County Historical Society.)

This Sunoco Station, pictured sometime in the 1940s, was on Persimmon Hill (6 Front Street), Boiling Springs. "Babe" Lutz was the owner. He later added a frozen custard stand next door. It was nicknamed "the Nest" by high school students in the late 1950s because all the "old geezers" hung out there. It was sold in the 1960s to Bill Gouse. There is a pizza shop in this location now.

Walter G. Arnold owned Arnold Motors Incorporated. It was located at 1201 Carlisle Springs Road, Carlisle. The main building is still standing and is directly across from the Carlisle Fairgrounds, owned by Carlisle Events. Carlisle Events is recognized as one of the country's largest automotive show promoters. (Both, courtesy Thomas Fraker.)

Walter Arnold built his first service station in 1938 and was an Esso dealer. An automobile dealership building was added in 1946, which was the beginning of his Desoto-Plymouth relationship. Around 1960, he gave up the Desoto franchise and became a Pontiac dealer. Eventually, he also took on an International Truck dealership, which operated at the same location. (Courtesy Thomas Fraker.)

John E. Minich was the proprietor of this 1950s-era Gulf station. Minich and his son Ellsworth operated three different Gulf stations in Cumberland County, spanning a total of 45 years. This location was 329 Hanover Street, Carlisle. (Courtesy John Minich.)

Station owner John E. Minich (seated) and his son Ellsworth "Ellsey" Minich (right), along with an employee, listen to a Gulf sales representative explain some new products and promotions. The Minich stations were always well-kept and neat. (Courtesy of John Minich.)

Ellsey Minich shows a special check to his employees. The dealership won a promotional contest sponsored by Gulf. The prize was this $25,000 check. A good portion of the money was used to buy a new Chevrolet tow truck. (Courtesy John Minich.)

This station was located at 7034 Carlisle Pike, Silver Spring Township. From its opening in 1969, it was operated under the Kayo brand until it was purchased and rebranded by Hess in 1983. (Courtesy Cumberland County Historical Society.)

This grouping of gas pumps, a used car lot, and a restaurant was located at 1712–1714 Hummel Avenue, Camp Hill. In the 1940s, the restaurant/bar at 1712 Hummel Avenue was known as the White Hill Café; it is still in operation. In 2021, one of the original buildings at 1714 Hummel Avenue was completely destroyed by fire. (Courtesy West Shore Historical Society.)

Identifying the locations of various buildings was made easier if the proprietor's name was prominently displayed in the photograph. A search for "Ed Jerore" in an early Cumberland County phone book revealed his location at Third Street and Bosler Avenue, Lemoyne.

For decades, the Lemoyne Auto Shop, located on the northeast corner of Third and Market Streets in Lemoyne, was a landmark of the West Shore. Several major routes converged in this location, as hinted by the AAA signs on the lower left. At the time of this photograph, there were only two road bridges spanning the Susquehanna River into Harrisburg, and choosing either one of them would have taken many travelers right past this garage. (Courtesy West Shore Historical Society.)

This attendant is flanked by two identical clock-face gas pumps from the 1930s. Above the Atlantic Refining logo is a small rectangular plate. It resembles a car license plate mounted on the pump. These are Pennsylvania fuel permits, each with a unique number, fabricated just like a vehicle license plate. These have a date of 1937. Automobile dealerships were seen as experts in all things car-related. This expertise extended to gas, with customers believing that the dealership would know the best type of gas for their specific car. Both images are at the same location (King and Fayette Streets, Shippensburg) but at different time periods.

This area is known as the "Lemoyne Bottleneck" due to the amount of traffic congestion during the day. The Market Street bridge is in the background. This was an important clue in helping to determine the location of this photograph.

Ford Motor Company

CHESTER, PA.

FACTORY AND GENE
DEARBORN

October 22 1940

1940 OCT 24 AM 8 05

Mr L B Smith
c/o L B Smith Motor Co
Lemoyne Pennsylvania

Dear Mr Smith:

It is with considerable pleasure that we enclose herewith copy of the Ford Sales Agreement which you recently signed with us.

We are looking forward to a permanent and profitable relationship as together we work out the business available to us because of this agreement. Along this line, we offer to you for your use the entire facilities of the organizatioh at this Branch, and suggest that at no time need you hesitate to call upon us.

With every good wish for the success of your business, we are

Very truly yours,
FORD MOTOR COMPANY

C. J. Snyffer

Branch Manager

CJS G

With two decades of experience under his belt remanufacturing and selling used vehicles, Luther Bruce Smith opened this beautiful "motorport" at 1100 Market Street, Lemoyne, in 1941. (Pictured at left is a copy of the franchise agreement.) The building comprised a new car showroom, used car sales, a service garage, and Esso gasoline. More than 80 years later, L.B. Smith Ford Lincoln is still a leader in new and used car sales and service—but one has to look elsewhere if they only want a fill-up. (Both, courtesy West Shore Historical Society.)

This late-1950s Gulf station was located at the triangle in West Fairview, along Routes 11 and 15 at Second Street. A small sign above the doorway revealed the owner (Sheetz Bros.). The building is no longer there; it is just an empty lot.

This Sunoco Filling Station was at Fourth and Market Streets in Lemoyne. Thomas and Zedna Commella signed a lease with the Sun Oil Company on March 30, 1939. Next to the station was Boyd Motor Company, which provided sales and service for Ford vehicles. (Courtesy Warrenette Sprenkle and the West Shore Historical Society.)

An early-1950s image of Three Gables in Camp Hill (at Thirty-Second and Market Streets) shows two of its trusty service vehicles. All service stations had a tow truck, and many had a three-wheel utility motorcycle, or "trike." Harley-Davidson was well-known for these specialty vehicles called Servi-Cars, which could be used to deliver parts or aid in picking up a customer's car. It could be tethered to the rear bumper of a car and safely transported back to the repair garage.

It was not uncommon for a busy intersection to have gas stations at all four corners. Kernan and Bard's Atlantic station was one of four at Thirty-Second and Market Streets, Camp Hill.

Four

Full Service in York and Lancaster Counties

The Lincoln Highway was the first designated and improved transcontinental highway in the United States. Beginning in 1921, the Lincoln Highway Garage (at East Market and Harrison Streets, York) offered services to travelers along the famed highway. After 83 years, the garage sold its last gasoline in May 2004. The building was torn down, and a new Turkey Hill convenience store was constructed. There had been an appeal by the Pennsylvania Lincoln Highway Association for Turkey Hill to preserve the historic building. While no parts of the original building remain, there is a mural and a few vintage gas pumps on display as a reminder of its history. (Courtesy York County History Center.)

Romeo D'Agostino immigrated to the United States from Italy at age 12. He opened his first Atlantic Refining service station and body shop before age 30. The location was 118 Old York Road, New Cumberland (Fairview Township). His service garage was close to the New Cumberland Army Depot, and he did a lot of service work for the government. D'Agostino was able to purchase a variety of government surplus items over the years. Some items were for use in his business (lumber). Other items were to be repaired and resold. One year, he bought four full-sized tanks. His son John fondly remembers driving one around the property crushing old cars with it. (Courtesy John D'Agostino.)

This was Romeo's D'Agostino's second service station, at 118 Old York Road, New Cumberland (Fairview Township). It was the same location as the first building but a more elaborate complex. He and his wife, Miriam, lived upstairs with their children. In addition to being a service station, there was a lunch counter and dance hall in the back of the building. It was a popular hangout for GIs stationed at the New Cumberland Army Depot and the ladies they met there. D'Agostino would receive Christmas cards for years from couples who got married after meeting there. In 1959, the location became the first Karns, a local grocery store chain. (Courtesy John D'Agostino.)

Romeo D'Agostino, with assistance from his young daughter Carol (D'Agostino) Spagnolo, fills up a 1940 Willys automobile. The 1945 license plate is from Michigan, likely a driver who is stationed nearby at the New Cumberland Army Depot. (Courtesy John D'Agostino.)

ROMEO'S SERVICE STATION
INTERSECTION
YORK AND LEWISBERRY HIGHWAYS

No. 26

LEMOYNE, PA. 6/18 1938

PAY TO THE ORDER OF Atlantic Refining Company $61.96/100

Sixty one 96/100 DOLLARS

ROMEO'S SERVICE STATION

WEST SHORE NATIONAL BANK
OF LEMOYNE
60-1748 LEMOYNE, PA. 60-1748

Romeo D'Agostino

Besides photographs, the D'Agostino family has a few other souvenirs from their service station past. This canceled check, written to Atlantic Refining Company, is from 1938. (Courtesy John D'Agostino.)

This is an excellent example of a neighborhood service station being conveniently located next door to a grocery store. A service station customer could walk safely to Food Fair and do the grocery shopping while their car was being serviced. The Food Fair chain began operation in 1927 and evolved from a small grocery store in Harrisburg. Its territory was primarily in the mid-Atlantic and southeastern United States. The location of this photograph was South George Street and West Boundary Avenue, York. (Courtesy York County History Center.)

Early car dealerships like Lefever Brothers (located at 116 North Baltimore Street, Dillsburg) were good for selling gas to the public. Dealerships were a one-stop shop for all car-related needs. Customers could buy a car, get it serviced, and fill up their gas tank all in one place. This made it convenient for customers, saving them time and effort.

Sinclair is famous for its dinosaur logo, and some stations even featured life-size dinosaur statues. In the 1930s and 1940s, the company adopted a more streamlined, Art Moderne style with smooth, rounded corners and horizontal lines. This was in line with the popular aesthetic of the time, which emphasized speed, efficiency, and modernity. This location was at 407 Baltimore Street, Hanover. (Courtesy York County History Center.)

This small Art Deco service station, sleek and modern for its time, sits in striking contrast with the imposing Western Maryland Railway passenger station to its rear, one of many grand designs by noted York architect John A. Dempwolf. Nothing remains of either building today. The Atlantic station was owned by Dale H. Stambaugh. The location is the northwest corner of North George and Arch Streets, York. (Courtesy Dan Stambaugh.)

Ralph C. Glatfelter retired in 1990 after 13 years as owner and operator of Dover Exxon. Prior to owning the Exxon, he was owner and operator for 10 years of Glatfelter's Gulf on North George Street in York. Shown here are photographs of Ralph Glatfelter and his Gulf service station. These are part of author Jimmy Rosen's Central Pennsylvania Gulf collection. A few years ago, Rosen was put in touch with Ralph's granddaughter Kristi, who had a grand opening flyer from her grandfather's Gulf station. Upon closer examination of the 1957 flyer, the two photographs in Rosen's collection were the actual photographs used for the flyer. It is amazing the pictures and the flyer came together 65 years later. (Both, courtesy Kristi Glatfelter.)

This is the original 1957 Gulf flyer announcing the grand opening of Glatfelter's new York service station. (Courtesy Kristi Glatfelter.)

Gas station owners started diversifying their offerings by adding convenience stores, car washes, and other services to their establishments. This allowed them to generate additional revenue streams and cater to customers' needs beyond just fuel. Publications like this May 1957 *Gulf News* would alert their dealers to some of these new opportunities.

Atlantic Refining offered words of advice to its franchise dealers in a 1949 booklet mailed to all of them: "Your station is always on display. To attract the motorist, it is first essential that it be neat and clean at all times. First impressions count—and the appearance of your business home reflects your habits and the quality of service and products you offer. Study your station from the other side of the street. Does it have a prosperous appearance? Is it clean and tidy? If you were a motorist, would you drive in?" This location was on South Queen Street in Spry, a suburb of York. This neat station appeared to heed the advice.

Williams Chevrolet was located along Route 230 in Elizabethtown and was built in 1957. Like many automobile dealerships at the time, it had full-service retail pumps. Gasoline sales added to the profits of the dealership. Additionally, attendants were in a good position to detect needed auto repairs, worn tires, and other issues and were quasi-salespeople for future car purchases. With the proliferation of self-service pumps and convenience stores, that competition helped put an end to gas outlets at most car dealerships.

On November 10, 1930, the largest tire in the world came rolling into York. This was a part of nationwide promotion for Goodyear Tire and Rubber Company. The location was Motor Tire Sales at 541 West Market Street. The date of the picture (1930) is written on the giant tire tread, and the car's license plate is dated 1930 as well. The business was owned by Lawrence Jacob Allen. An air meter was put out front for free public use. (Both, courtesy Mike Allen.)

Charles Harbold owned and operated Harbold's Esso service station on old Route 15 (709 Range End Road) in Dillsburg. There was also a small restaurant on-site. Harbold purchased the business around 1952 and enjoyed servicing the local community for many years. In the early years, Harbold's was open 24 hours daily to accommodate the heavy interstate traffic as Route 15 was not just a local road, it was a main route north and south. However, a new highway bypass opened that would impact business as it was no longer on the main road. The station had to cut back hours and close the small restaurant but still remained in business for many more years. (Courtesy Joanne Harbold Minich.)

A pizza shop now occupies this former Atlantic Refining station. It shows that original gas stations and repair garage buildings could be adapted to other types of businesses. This location is 299 West Market Street (old Route 30), Hallam. There are photographs inside of its early gas station history.

Charles Rudisill's first Gulf service station opened 67 years ago in 1957. It was located at Mount Rose Avenue and South Yale Street in Spring Garden Township, a suburb of York. Though no longer affiliated with Gulf, it still operates as a repair garage, and it is still owned by a Rudisill family member, daughter Lynne Spangler.

Shown here in his early 30s, Charles Rudisill had four Gulf locations at one time in York. His association with Gulf began in 1957. (This one was at 2301 East Market Street.) He always made sure his service stations were neatly kept. Though no longer affiliated with Gulf, one location remains and still operates as a repair garage. It is owned by his daughter, Lynne Spangler. (Courtesy Lynne Spangler.)

W.S. "Sylvester" Stuckey Sr. founded Stuckey's as a roadside pecan stand along Highway 23 in Eastman, Georgia, in 1937. Stuckey drove around the countryside and bought pecans from local farmers to sell at his stand, along with local honey and souvenirs. His wife, Ethel, added her delicious homemade candies—southern delicacies like pralines, divinities, and iconic pecan log rolls. Through grit and determination, the Stuckeys grew the stores from these humble beginnings to a roadside empire. At its peak in the 1960s, the little pecan company had become an integral part of the American road trip. It boasted 368 stores in over 30 states, with each offering kitschy souvenirs, clean restrooms, Texaco gas, and, of course, their famous candies. This former location was along Route 30, Ronks. It currently is a quilt store. (Courtesy Stephanie Stuckey.)

This is an early photograph of Miller's Smorgasbord, along Route 30, Ronks. Miller's began simply in 1929 as a gas station and repair garage. Although the gas pumps are long gone, Miller's will celebrate 95 years in 2024. (Courtesy Megan Weiss.)

The Lexington store (at 153 Chestnut Street, Lititz) was first opened in 1855 by Jacob Hershey. In 1894, a post office was added. The establishment was owned by several families throughout the decades and was well-stocked with groceries, household goods, and hunting supplies. In 1969, the store ceased operations and was converted into apartments. (Photograph from the Donmoyer family; courtesy Cory Van Brookhoven.)

Shown here is Jerry Adams, who owned and operated the Lincoln Avenue Garage and Mobiloil Station at the corner of North Cedar Street and Lincoln Avenue in Lititz. The pumps and repair shop are long gone, but the building remains. (Photograph from the Robert "Sketch" Mearig Collection; courtesy Cory Van Brookhoven, Lititz Historical Foundation.)

In 1920, Stephen Francis "S.F." Ulrich lived here (122 South Market Street, Elizabethtown) and was listed as an auto dealer. Ulrich operated a garage and auto storage facility with an Atlantic gas station across the street, just south of this location. In 1924, Lee Hassinger and Herman Risser opened the Hassinger & Risser dealership, specializing in selling Dodge, Chevrolet, Pontiac, Ford, auto parts, and service. (There was one gas pump along the curb.) By 1943, it was known as the H.S. Risser Motor Company. (Courtesy Jean-Paul Benowitz.)

S.F. Ulrich operated this gas station and garage at 233 South Market Street, Elizabethtown. Formerly a liquor dealer, in 1908 Ulrich opened the first Buick dealership in Elizabethtown. In 1915, Ulrich became a Dodge Brothers dealership as well. In 1929, when S.F. retired, his son Louis L. Ulrich established S.F. Ulrich Incorporated, expanding to include Chevrolet sales. (Courtesy Jean-Paul Benowitz.)

The Amoco gas station on North Market Street in Elizabethtown was part of R.H. Forney Chrysler-Plymouth. The right side of the building was used as a one-car dealership showroom. The Forney repair garage building was to the right, and it was set back several yards off North Market Street. All of Milton Hershey's personal vehicles were Chryslers, specially ordered by R.H. Forney. (Courtesy Jean-Paul Benowitz.)

This commercial building at 40 North Market Street, Elizabethtown was built around 1900 as an automobile mechanic garage. It served for nearly 50 years as part of the R.H. Forney Chrysler-Plymouth automobile dealership. Forney was one of the earliest national retail dealers for Chrysler-Plymouth. Since he was 16 years old, Forney designed, built, and raced sports cars. He also chauffeured people on road trips in the years prior to automobile ownership being commonplace. The showroom for Forney's dealership was south of Conoy Creek attached to the gas station owned by the Keller and, later, the Lutz families. (Courtesy Jean-Paul Benowitz.)

Originally opened by John G. Enterline as a carriage works, this building was taken over by son Morris K. Enterline in 1921 to sell and service automobiles when it became clear that motors were the way of the future. Morris later moved his operations to nearby Elizabethtown, and this building was razed in 1960. The automobile in the foreground is a 1934 Dodge limousine hearse. (Courtesy Elizabethtown Historical Society.)

Jacob Hoffman Garber Sr., a former tobacco dealer, owned this gas station and garage at 833–845 South Market Street. In 1915, Garber opened the first Ford dealership in Elizabethtown. Eventually, this became the Garber Ford Mercury dealership where Louis L. Ulrich trained in sales before joining his father, Stephen Francis Ulrich, establishing S.F. Ulrich Incorporated and selling Buick, Dodge, and Chevrolet. In 1928, Garber was one of the founders of the Elizabethtown Chamber of Commerce. (Courtesy Jean-Paul Benowitz.)

Five

Gas up in Franklin, Fulton, and Bedford Counties

Pictured is Robert Shively (left), founder of Shively Motors Inc., and driver Charles Greene (right) in front of Shively Motors in 1953. The car is a 1953 Dodge Coronet with the first Hemi engine in a Dodge called the Red Ram V-8. This was the beginning of Shively Motors' interest in racing. Later, Bud Faubel, vice president and general manager at the dealership, would go on to win many trophies during the 1960s as a factory driver for Dodge and win the 1965 Mr. Stock Eliminator title with his 1965 Dodge Coronet sponsored by Shively Motors. (Courtesy Bryan Burkholder.)

Pictured is the used car lot located across the street from Shively Motors in 1959. Shively Motors was originally founded in 1939 in Chambersburg, Pennsylvania, by Robert Shively with only the Dodge and Plymouth franchises. Shively Motors continued to expand and was known as the Auto Supermarket, carrying Chrysler, Imperial, Dodge, DeSoto, Plymouth, and Simca franchises as well as used cars and trucks. Shively Motors also was an Atlantic service station from the 1940s through the 1960s. (Courtesy Bryan Burkholder.)

Owen's Filling Station was located on the 1300 block of the Lincoln Highway (Route 30), Stoufferstown. Today, a modern Sheetz convenience store occupies the property, offering travelers a way to fill-up but with self-service pumps. With a few exceptions, the days of the true service station are in the past.

This foursome of mechanics appears ready for a variety of repairs and fill-ups. This was the era of full service. R.L. Patterson Atlantic was located at 438 Lincoln Way East, Chambersburg.

One of the earliest garages in Chambersburg was the Chambersburg Auto Company, started by D.G. Pfoutz in 1905. This location at 20–28 North Second Street was built in 1910 and sold Atlantic gasoline and motor oil. Pfoutz eventually became a sales representative for White, Franklin, Cadillac, and Studebaker automobiles.

An early Coca-Cola truck makes a delivery at this Texaco station, located at 1881 Philadelphia Avenue, Chambersburg.

E.S. Keefer set up shop at 609 Lincoln Way West (Route 30), Chambersburg. The building is still there, with a newer addition added. It has been a variety of businesses over the last 100 years. The latest is a tattoo shop.

William "Bill" Wakefield started Bill's Place on June 10, 1923, according to *Pittsburgh Press* writer Gilbert Love, who walked across the state in June 1962. Wakefield was quite a huckster and seemingly sold just about everything at his place. (He also served as a school director in the 1940s.) He started with a tower across the road but soon moved it adjacent to his place so that travelers could look out over Clear Valley, which Wakefield named. (Both, courtesy Brian Butko.)

BILL'S PLACE

BILLS PLACE, PA.

Adding Cheer All the Year

---

13 GAS PUMPS

Efficient Service on all Lubrication. We have the proper Grade of Oil and Grease for any car.

Try Our "Backhouse" for Comfort

Cove Mountain Tea Room sat on a tight curve along Route 30 (Lincoln Highway) east of McConnellsburg. It was just downhill from Tuscarora Summit. It later was known as Forrester's Place. Though down from the hilltop, where most drivers stopped for the view, it was still a popular stop for buses. The garage later became an antique store. (Courtesy of Brian Butko.)

Larry's Place, on Route 30 in Everett, went through many owners and name changes. Other names were River View Park, Sherm's, and Gene's. It was destroyed when the ramps were built east of Everett for the Route 30 bypass. (Courtesy Brian Butko.)

In the early days of gasoline sales, one could find multiple fuel brands at one location. This is a phenomenon that does not occur today, but it was very much part of this location 90 years ago. This was Long View Lodge atop Scrub Ridge Summit west of McConnellsburg. It endures as Tower Ridge Inn. (Courtesy Brian Butko.)

Based in Hagerstown, Maryland, this is one of the few H.L. Mills gas stations in Pennsylvania. The location was 105 Lincoln Way West, Chambersburg. It was directly across from the popular Texas Hot Lunch. (Courtesy Franklin County Historical Society.)

It was hard to travel far along the Lincoln Highway without finding a service station. Many of them had late hours and were even open 24 hours to accommodate travelers. This one was located at 700 Lincoln Way West, Chambersburg.

Frank R. Keller owned and operated West Point Service Station (Lincoln Way West and West Loudon Streets, Chambersburg). In a 1928 Chambersburg newspaper article, the writer describes Keller as "an all-around man, a man who can always be counted upon to do his best, and as a result he is building a splendid business at the West Point Service Station."

Six

Top Off the Tank in Perry, Juniata, Snyder, and Northumberland Counties

At the intersection of Routes 104 and 35 in Snyder County stands the former Landis Texaco Service Station, built in 1931 by Lester Landis. The Mount Pleasant Mills station not only provided gas and oil, but also served as a convenience store offering small goods, tobacco products, candy, soda, and Hershey's ice cream. Lester died in 1957, leaving ownership to his son Ardell, who operated the station until it closed in 1980. In 1997, it was purchased by Lester's grandsons Gary and Kenneth Pyle, saving it from demolition by a bank firm that had interest in the corner lot property. In the following years, it has served as a restaurant under various management and is currently known as Cruiser's Café. This image portrays a typical scene from the station's prime in the 1950s. Gary Pyle can be seen as the Texaco attendant at the pumps. Others on the bench are, from left to right, Bob Roush, Gard Zechman, and Edwin Moyer. (Photograph by Irvin Hoover; courtesy Angie Pyle.)

This c. 1970 photograph shows a teenage Steve Landis pumping gas at his father Ardell's station. His ride was a 1957 Chevrolet two-door hardtop. (Courtesy Angie Pyle.)

Lester Landis, proprietor of Landis's Texaco station in Mount Pleasant Mills, is standing proudly in front of his Texaco Sky Chief gas pump. Sky Chief was introduced in 1938 as a high-octane premium fuel. (Courtesy Angie Pyle.)

Many early car dealers had retail gas pumps. Dealerships could use gas sales as a promotional tool, offering discounts on gas to customers who bought cars from them. This attracted more customers and increased overall sales. This Northumberland Ford dealer, Mertz Motor Company (367 Front Street), had three pumps along the curb in this 1930s photograph.

The W.E. Schlegel garage was located in the center of Thompsontown. This 1920s real-photo postcard shows six gas pumps out front greeting customers on their way to Selinsgrove and Sunbury. A large repair garage was in the back. Today, the building is a pizza shop, but it retains the original style. (Courtesy of Glenda Pyle.)

The Amity Hall Inn in Watts Township, Perry County, was a rest stop for weary travelers since its construction around 1810 near the confluence of the Susquehanna and Juniata Rivers. By the mid-20th century, the old brick tavern was expanded into a multipurpose complex, serving not only overnight guests, but also those just passing through. Seen here is the Amity Hall Lunch, a small outbuilding offering a quick meal, washrooms, fuel, and maps.

R.G. Beaver was a former hardware store in Millerstown, and this is the only known photograph of it showing gas pumps out front. The address is 10 North Market Street. The proprietor, Ralph G. Beaver, was a direct descendant of Pennsylvania governor James Beaver, also from Millerstown. At one time, Governor Beaver served on the board of trustees of the Pennsylvania State University. The football stadium, Beaver Stadium, is named after him.

The Ranch House restaurant was opened in 1949 by the Deiter family. There were Gulf-brand gas pumps as well. Due to a widening of the highway (Routes 11 and 15), ownership had to relocate the pumps. Eventually, the family got out of the retail fuel business and concentrated solely on the restaurant. The Ranch House will celebrate 75 years in business in 2024. (Courtesy the Ranch House.)

After the new three-lane highway was completed, the Ranch House gas pumps had to be relocated due to the widening of the roadway. They were moved toward the lower end of the parking lot, making them less convenient. Eventually, they were removed altogether, with the concentration being on the restaurant. The Ranch House will celebrate 75 years in 2024. (Courtesy the Ranch House.)

Robert "Bob" Kisner purchased 81 South Main Street, Duncannon, in 1962, where he owned and operated Kisner's Texaco Station, along with his wife, Charlotte (pictured), and son Robert "Bobby". While the concept was not yet mainstream, Kisner's Texaco featured a convenience store complete with hot sandwiches and a selection of groceries. Following the removal of the gas pumps in the 1980s, the business continued operating as Kisner's Garage, a full-service garage with repairs, state inspections, towing, and a junkyard. Bob's love for antique cars was evident, as his collection grew to include a 1929 Elcar, a 1930 Ford Model A, a 1920 Ford Model T, a 1917 International delivery truck, a 1929 Chevrolet pickup, and others. Friends and families could view the collection during any of the various local parades they were entered into. Kisner's Garage was a place of gathering; many stories were told by many people sitting around the wood stove in the back of the garage or on one of the benches that sat out front. Bob, Charlotte, and Bobby have all passed, but the memories and stories surrounding Kisner's Garage will live on. (Courtesy of Tricia Kisner Shaffer.)

Pictured is Jennie Campbell. This Campbell-owned service station was located between Newport and Millerstown along old Route 22. The actual address is 312 West Juniata Parkway. (Courtesy of the Campbell family.)

Bruaw's Bar-B-Q was located along the Susquehanna Trail (Route 11) south of Liverpool. This 90-year-old photograph is another example of an enterprising proprietor combining gas pumps with a restaurant, making it convenient for the traveler to have a good meal and top off their tank at one location. (Courtesy Art Bruaw.)

This 1930s photograph shows the front of the T.H. Hoffman Tire Shop, located on South High Street, Duncannon. This building as well as all of the other structures on South High Street were razed for the construction of Routes 11 and 15. Pictured are Thomas H. Hoffman and his grandson Carl Gault. Hoffman was an avid coon hunter, and pictured are two of his many hounds. (Courtesy Duane Hammaker.)

The 1935 image above was originally published in *Got Gas?*; the location and people are unknown. The negative was cropped in such a way as to hide the important clues above the doorway. Soon after *Got Gas?* was released, a copy was purchased by Chuck Sekulski, who recognized the unknown photograph on page 67; the people in it were his father, uncles, and grandparents. The mystery was solved—it was Sunbury. Pictured below, the 1936 flood was a setback for Sekulski's new Atlantic service station, which opened in 1935. (Above, courtesy Jimmy Rosen; below, courtesy Chuck Sekulski.)

This Atlantic station was part of the Sekulski family for decades and was located on Front Street in Sunbury. The Sekulski family has graciously shared several original pictures for this book, including the cover photograph. (Courtesy Chuck Sekulski.)

Promotions were a big part of early service stations. This Sekulski flyer advertised its 26th anniversary open house in 1961. Customers received modest gifts with a fuel purchase. (Courtesy Chuck Sekulski.)

The Keystone Inn was located between Newport and Millerstown at 312 West Juniata Parkway, which was along old Route 22. Early tourist inns, motor courts, and cottages sold gasoline as a convenience to their guests. During the early 20th century, when automobile travel was becoming more popular, these establishments were often located in rural or remote areas where gas stations were uncommon. This also provided additional income for the owners. (Courtesy the Campbell family.)

Foster and Charles Cupp opened Cupp Brothers Ford at 114 North Main Street, Mifflintown, in 1921. By 1926, they had become so successful that they joined with their other brothers, Oscar and Harvey, to open Cupp Motor Company in Lewistown, obtaining the contract to sell Fords there as well.

Seven

Out of Gas

This chapter contains photographs of still unidentified locations. They remain lost, but the one common denominator is that they are all in central Pennsylvania; however, there are not enough clues to pinpoint their exact address. This photograph shows a Coca-Cola sign with "New-York Tourist Camp" wording boldly printed on it. It is not in New York (there is a hyphen between "New" and "York"), so the thought is possibly a "New" location in York, Pennsylvania. There is a Neuman's ice cream sign (lower left), which was manufactured in York. With Route 30 (Lincoln Highway) passing through the York area with many out-of-state travelers, this tourist camp could be along that roadway.

This 1920s location continues to remain anonymous. Normally, large rooftop signs offer better address clues. This sign has no proprietor name or town mentioned. There are no distinguishable buildings around it to provide a hint either.

These smiling gentlemen stand in front of an unidentified Atlantic Refining location. There are book photographs of similar buildings with proprietors' names above the doorways or clues in the windows. The way this photograph was cropped, all meaningful clues were lost.

There are no address clues in this photograph, and the surrounding buildings offer no help either. A Burdan's ice cream sidewalk sign (lower-right center) suggests the Harrisburg area, as there was a manufacturing plant at Twenty-Fifth and Derry Streets.

This modest gas station building offers no clues to its exact address. A blurry poster in the window may have helped, but it is unreadable. The location was on a trolley route, but so much of central Pennsylvania was at that time. Acto gasoline was sold at many locations so that does not narrow down this spot. For now, this Standard Oil Company of Pennsylvania filling station remains anonymous.